HOSEA

HIS REDEEMING LOVE

10 Publishing
a division of 10 of those.com

First published in Great Britain in 2015

British Library Cataloguing in Publication Data

A record for this book is available from the British Library

ISBN: 978-1-910587-16-4

Designed by Diane Bainbridge

Printed in the UK

10Publishing, a division of 10ofthose.com
9D Centurion Court, Farington, Leyland, PR25 3UQ, England
Email: info@10ofthose.com
Website: www.10ofthose.com

David Gibb

31 UNDATED DEVOTIONS THROUGH THE BOOK OF HOSEA

AN OVERVIEW

1:1 tells us when Hosea ministered: 'during the reigns of [kings] Uzziah, Jotham, Ahaz and Hezekiah, kings of Judah, and during the reign of Jeroboam the son of Joash king of Israel'. So this is the middle of the eighth century BC. Israel had been torn into two kingdoms (Israel and Judah). While Amos ministers to the southern kingdom of Judah, Hosea chiefly speaks to the northern kingdom of Israel. Israel is at peace and prosperous but the mighty Assyria, over in the east, is gathering strength and beginning to move ever closer to them. As we read the book we discover all is not right within Israel either. The people have forgotten God and have gone after Baal, a local fertility god who promised bumper harvests. So Hosea is sent by God to warn his people and to woo them back to him.

It's Hosea, more than any other of the Old Testament books, which shows us that God loves his people as passionately and as jealously as a devoted husband loves his wife. And the prophet gets not only to say this but to live it, for in the tragedy of his own struggling marriage he learns how God feels towards his unfaithful people.

In the structure of the book we see the parallel story between Hosea's marriage to Gomer and God's marriage to his people:

1:1 – 3:5 ***Hosea and his bride:*** the heartbreaking story of Hosea and his wife, Gomer.

4:1 – 11:11 ***God and his bride (Part 1):*** Hosea's story is seen to be a poor reflection of the story of God and his bride, Israel.

11:12 – 14:9 ***God and his bride (Part 2):*** God's anger towards his unfaithful bride is highlighted, but so too are the early days of the relationship, when all was good. There is a plea to return and a promise of blessing.

KEY VERSE

'The LORD said to me, "Go, show your love to your wife again, though she is loved by another and is an adulteress. Love her as the LORD loves the Israelites, though they turn to other gods and love the sacred raisin cakes"' (Hos. 3:1).

DAY 1

READ Hosea 1:1–3

Like the other prophets, Hosea begins (v. 1) by telling us when he spoke God's Word to the nation. (Read 2 Kgs. 14 - 20 which tell you about the kings mentioned.)

Verse 2 comes as a huge shock! God commands Hosea to go and marry a prostitute, or literally 'a wife of whoredom'. Can God really be saying this? Adultery was listed in the Ten Commandments as a disgraceful act that demanded God's judgment (Ex. 20:14). Yet here is God's own messenger being told by him to marry an immoral woman. Why?

God gives the reason: 'because the land is guilty of the vilest adultery in departing from the LORD.' In other words, the pain that Hosea would feel as he tried to love a woman who was continually unfaithful was just a picture of the pain God felt in trying to love a people who continually went after other 'lovers' or 'gods'.

Have you ever thought about how God feels towards you? We say a lot about what God thinks and what he says, but Hosea is going to show us God's feelings. God feels passionately about his people. When the New Testament talks about Christ purchasing the church to be his bride (Acts 20:28; Eph. 5:25–27; Rev. 19:7–9), it is no accident. God loves us deeply, and every time we flirt with sin or substitute God for something or someone else, we hurt the One to whom we are bound.

So this is a love story. Verse 3 tells us that Hosea marries Gomer. He will not just preach God's message to the people; he will have to live it out within his own family. He will know the pain and heartache of loving but receiving no love in return.

A PRAYER

Heavenly Father, as I read this love story please rekindle my love for you and my commitment to you. In Christ, who loved and gave himself for me. Amen.

DAY 2

READ Hosea 1:4–11

The footballer David Beckham called his son 'Harper Seven', the actress Gywneth Paltrow called her daughter 'Apple', and the musician Frank Zappa named his daughter 'Moon Unit'! Yet none of these is as shocking as the names God now tells Hosea to give his children. With each name we see how hurt God is by his people's spiritual adultery, and that he will act in response to it.

Hosea's first son will be called 'Jezreel' (v. 4) after the place where an entire royal house of Israel had been butchered (2 Kgs. 9:21 – 10:11). It was meant to shock and to warn Israel of what God was about to do!

Gomer again gives birth, this time to a daughter (v. 6). She will bear the terrible name 'Lo-Ruhamah', which means 'not loved' or (more literally) 'no compassion'. (The same Hebrew word is translated as 'compassion' in Isaiah 49:15: 'Can a mother forget the baby at her breast and have no compassion on the child she has borne?') That Lo-Ruhamah is given this shocking name shows how God felt about his people. Their sin had so hurt him that he would no longer love or forgive them.

Most devastating of all is the name of the last child, another son: 'Lo-Ammi' which means 'not my people' (v. 8). Yet God had said to Moses, 'I will take you as my own people and I will be your God' (Ex. 6:7). Could this really be the end?

Yet, just when all seems lost, God speaks again. In verse 10 we discover the promise to Abraham of a vast people (Gen. 15:5) is *still* on track! In verse 11 the promise to King David of a united people with one king (2 Sam. 7) is *still* on track too! And God also promises: 'great will be the day of Jezreel'. Yes, Jezreel stood for bloody massacre, but the word also means 'God sows'. So Jezreel is *both* a warning of judgment *and* a promise of a future harvest.

Hosea didn't know how God would hold those two declarations together, but one day God's Son would hang on a cross and there God's anger and faithfulness would meet. Jesus would be shown 'no compassion' and become a nobody, all so that we could become his people and receive his mercy. Look up 1 Peter 2:10 and marvel at God's faithfulness!

A PRAYER

Heavenly Father, thank you that because of Jesus I can be your child and know mercy. Amen.

DAY 3

READ Hosea 2:1–13

Chapter 2 opens with God, like an aggrieved husband, at the court filing charges for divorce! Verse 2 reads: 'Rebuke your mother, rebuke her, for she is not my wife, and I am not her husband.' In verses 3–4 we see how far things have deteriorated between God and his people, and as he speaks we realise how strongly he feels about it – as he threatens to strip them of everything he had given them and to leave them with absolutely nothing, exposed and ashamed.

Israel had said, 'I will go after my lovers, who give me my food and my water, my wool and my linen, my oil and my drink' (v. 5). They thought they had got all they had by their own cleverness, but in verses 9–13 God effectively says, 'That's where you're wrong!' These things weren't Israel's at all, but God's. He had given them to Israel out of his love, and he could just as easily remove them from the Israelites.

We hear God's pain in verse 8: 'She has not acknowledged that I was the one who gave her the grain, the new wine and oil, who lavished on her the silver and gold – which they used for Baal.' Like a husband who has given a keepsake to his wife only to find she has given it to another man, God feels cheated by his people going after foreign gods. No wonder he cannot bring himself to speak directly to his wife, Israel (vv. 2–4). How does this help us to understand how God feels about our spiritual adultery?

God had gone to great lengths to rescue his people and provide for them, and under King Jeroboam II they had become very rich. Yet Israel had '"decked herself with rings and jewellery, and went after her lovers, but me she forgot," declares the LORD' (v. 13). That's the danger of material prosperity. Moses had warned of this (read Deut. 8:10–14, 19). We too think we're in control and we don't need God anymore. God is issuing his people a final warning in verses 2–3: stop being unfaithful or I will take everything from you. We need to take heed of this.

A PRAYER

Heavenly Father, show me where in my life I have forgotten you. Help me to turn from that attitude. In your mercy. Amen.

DAY 4

READ Hosea 2:14–23

'Therefore', says God in verse 14, 'I am now going to ...' What would you expect God to say after all that he's poured out in verses 1–13? Perhaps 'I am now going to ... destroy you'? Or 'wipe you off the face of the earth'? Or 'humiliate you'? But no, look at what he actually says: 'Therefore I am now going to allure her; I will lead her into the desert and speak tenderly to her. There I will give her back her vineyards, and will make the Valley of Achor a door of hope.'

How astonishing! Yes, Israel will be stripped and will go back into the desert (v. 3), but notice how tender this scene is. This will also be an opportunity to rekindle Israel's first love. God is going to turn the valley of trouble (which is what 'Achor' means) into 'a door of hope'. We can imagine Hosea anticipates Israel will look back at all the troubles God is about to bring on them and will say, 'Though it hurt me, it was good for me, because it led me back to him.' (Read Heb. 12:4–11 to find out why God sometimes disciplines us.)

The desert would be hard, but it could be an opportunity too. Verses 6–23 tell us what God intends to do there. It will lead to a disillusionment with idols (vv. 6–7). God will have us back even when our motivation is pretty self-centred! It will result in a new devotion (v. 16) as God's people discover that, unlike Baal, God is not a cruel tyrant/master but a loving 'husband'. There will be a new harmony (v. 18) as peace between God and his people ripples out. There will be a new justice (v. 19) as God comes laden with this and other betrothal gifts. And along with a new intimacy (v. 20) with God, there will be a new prosperity (vv. 21–22) and even a new restatement of the marriage vows (v. 23).

Would you have guessed that a chapter which begins as it does would end this way? What does that tell you about God?

A PRAYER

Lord God, I know that sometimes you have to take me through trouble, and even remove things from me to bring me back to you. Help me to see this trouble as a door of hope. For Christ's sake. Amen.

DAY 5

READ Hosea 3:1–2

Marriages are easy to break; it's mending them that's so hard, especially when adultery is involved. Chapter 3 tells the story of how Hosea has to learn to love his wife, despite her unfaithfulness.

Hosea is told by God to 'Go, show your love to your wife again, though she is loved by another and is an adulteress' (v. 1). Notice that Hosea is to 'go'. He must take the initiative, make the first move, even though he is the 'wronged' party. Notice too how Hosea is to go 'again'. Despite his wife's infidelities, her constant affairs, Hosea must persist in his love. Literally God says, 'love your wife'; it is a command. Perhaps by this stage Hosea no longer felt any love for her, but reconciling love is a love that goes again and again, in spite of feelings.

Hosea is also to love Gomer even though she doesn't love him! Look again at verse 1: 'Love her *as* the LORD loves the Israelites, though they turn to other gods and love the sacred raisin cakes' (my italics). God knows Israel doesn't love him. He knows they prefer the other gods and raisin cakes (the little delicacies they ate at the festivals to Baal). Yet God persists in loving Israel, and so too must Hosea love Gomer.

Astonishingly, Hosea will also have to buy his own wife back! Verse 2 tells us, 'So I bought her for fifteen shekels of silver and about a homer and a lethek of barley.' It looks like Gomer had run up debts and she'd had to sell herself into slavery. Yet Hosea swallows his injured pride and pays her debts – and then opens his arms to Gomer again (3:3). It costs him everything.

In Hosea's love for Gomer, we see a reflection of God's astonishing love for you and me. God has taken the initiative: seeking us and saving us. He has forgiven us despite our unfaithfulness. He knows how fickle our love for him is, and at huge cost – by sending his son Jesus to the cross – he has 'redeemed' us, that is, bought us back.

A PRAYER

Thank you, dear Father, that we were not redeemed with perishable things such as silver and gold but with the precious blood of Christ. Help us to see that cost and to ever be thankful. Amen.

DAY 6

READ Hosea 3:2–5

Our world is obsessed with quick answers – instant coffee, instant photography, instant messaging – but some things cannot be fixed in an instant. Hosea's marriage was one of them. If it was to heal it would take time and patience.

Hosea understood that: 'Then I told her, "You are to live with me for many days; you must not be a prostitute or be intimate with any man, and I will live with you"' (v. 3). As the prophet opens his arms to Gomer again, he tells her not to play around anymore. And he adds, 'I will live with you', or literally 'I will wait for you'. He will wait to be intimate with her again. He would make love to her when she really was committed to him, and not before. That would require real patience.

That's an important lesson for us when so few people are willing to wait to have sex these days. Hosea is showing us it takes time to grow to love someone deeply, and God's purpose is that sex should be the consummation of that intimacy, not a short cut to it.

Hosea begins to understand that God exercises patience too. Look at verses 4–5:

For the Israelites will live for many days without king or prince, without sacrifice or sacred stones, without ephod or idol. Afterwards the Israelites will return and seek the LORD their God and David their king. They will come trembling to the LORD and to his blessings in the last days.

Hosea sees dark days ahead for Israel: the monarchy and their religious life will fall. For a long time they'll have nothing, but one day, in the last days, a new king will come and then a new people of God will arise. They will be a people who will be repentant, seeking God, reverent and longing to know him and his blessings. Thank God that he was willing to exercise patience in sending his Son, and that we, by faith, are now able to live our lives in reverent fear and enjoy his blessing.

A PRAYER

Lord God, thank you that you do not wash your hands of us. Thank you for waiting for me to return to you. Help me to stay with you. In Christ's name. Amen.

DAY 7

READ Hosea 4:1–9

The story of Hosea's marriage now gives way to the second part of the prophecy: the even more heartbreaking account of Israel's unfaithfulness to the Lord. In chapter 4 we begin to see just how far this adultery has spread.

The scene opens with God taking his people to court (v. 1). His accusation is that: 'There is no faithfulness, no love, no acknowledgment of God', and the crimes he lists in verse 2 are straight from the Ten Commandments!

Religious decay spawns moral decay and then leads to environmental decay (v. 3). God had said, 'if you defile the land, it will vomit you out as it vomited out the nations that were before you' (Lev. 18:28). So as the land, wildlife, birdlife and sealife all began to die, nature itself chimed in with Hosea's preaching! Rejecting God does not lead to life, but to death.

And what about Israel's religious leaders? Were they helping? Verses 4–5 give us the shocking truth. God says, 'my people are destroyed from lack of knowledge' (v. 6). And why? Because the priests 'have ignored the law of your God'. Their job was to teach God's law to the people, but they'd stopped that! So the nation was completely unaware of what it meant to know and follow God.

But notice also how the priests 'feed on the sins of my people, and relish their wickedness' (v. 8). They encouraged sin! As Hosea says in verse 7, 'they exchanged their Glory for something disgraceful'. God was supposed to be their Glory, but instead the priests encouraged idol worship, and were doing a roaring trade out of it!

No wonder the number of priests had grown (v. 7), but looks can be deceptive, for God proclaims: 'The more the priests increased, the more they sinned against me'. So what will God do? 'Like people, like priests. I will punish both of them for their ways and repay them for their deeds' (v. 9).

Sadly, each step in Israel's decline could be traced back to verse 1.

A PRAYER

Heavenly Father, please may I be faithful, love you and know you today. May my church leaders not ignore your Word or encourage sin. In Christ's name. Amen.

DAY 8

READ Hosea 4:10–19

God has had enough. In this imaginary law court he is exposing Israel's crimes.

Hosea now presents evidence for Israel's unfaithfulness. Verse 11 begins and verse 14 ends with proverbs about Israel's lack of understanding. Sandwiched in-between are the things that have made them foolish: drunkenness (v. 11), consulting idols for guidance (v. 12) and offering sacrifices at the hilltop pagan shrines (v. 13).

The men went up to these 'shady' places (v. 13) to offer 'worship' to the god Baal in the form of sex with a shrine prostitute (v. 14). It was supposed to encourage Baal to make the crops grow. Was it any wonder that the younger generation were turning to sexual immorality?

But notice how God will not punish the teenage daughters for their lifestyle or the wives for their affairs (v. 14); it's the men he will hold responsible. They thought they could indulge in their drunken orgies and there would be no consequences, but all around them were the sad results in the unfaithfulness of their children and in the instability of their children's marriages. Perhaps that's why Jesus had more time for adulteresses and prostitutes than he did for Pharisees.

So in verse 15 Hosea turns to Israel's sister nation, Judah, and he says in effect, 'Watch out that you don't catch Israel's idolatry and immorality, or you'll be next in the dock! And watch out for Israel's religion too!' Gilgal and Bethel were two of Israel's shrines, but 'Bethel' (which meant 'house of God') has now become 'Beth Aven' ('house of evil'). So Hosea is essentially warning Judah: 'Keep away from places of worship like that! Even their liturgy has become corrupt: they can't even say, "As surely as the LORD lives" without it sounding like a fertility chant!'

Finally, in verse 16, Hosea adds an admonition along the lines of, 'Watch out for Israel's obstinacy!' God longs to be a shepherd to them, but like a stubborn bull they won't budge. Tragically, for a people like Israel, there can be only one end: 'A whirlwind will sweep them away, and their sacrifices will bring them shame' (v. 19).

What a warning! God *is* love, but he is not soft! If we resist God and dig our heels in, it will not end well.

A PRAYER

Heavenly Father, help me to have true understanding, and so live to please you. In the name of Christ. Amen.

DAY 9

READ Hosea 5:1–7

It was Elton John who sang, 'Sorry seems to be the hardest word', and it is. Imagine a husband deserts his wife for someone else, but in the end returns home. Their marriage will never recover unless the husband learns to say 'sorry', genuinely, from the heart. Hosea knew what it was to wait for his wife Gomer's apology, and God knew it too as he waited to hear that word of remorse on the lips of his bride, Israel.

Chapter 5 is all about a God who will exercise astonishing patience as he waits for that moment of contrition (see 5:15). We see too, in verses 1–7, the first step God takes in order to get his people to that point.

Verse 6 tells us how God will deliberately withdraw himself from Israel. He knows the best way to deal with stubborn sinners sometimes is to let us feel the emptiness and loneliness of a world without him. Israel may go to seek him as they take their sacrifices, but they won't find him.

Why? Look at verse 1: 'Hear this, you priests! Pay attention, you Israelites! Listen, O royal house! This judgment is against you'. God is basically saying, 'It's no good you priests blaming the kings, and the kings blaming the people – you are *all* to blame!' Mizpah and Tabor (traditional shrines) had simply become traps to get everyone to worship Baal. And it was no good Israel thinking they could bluff their way out of it (v. 3) for God could read them like a book. People may have thought that they could turn back to God eventually, but it doesn't work like that. Sin does not permit us to return to God (v. 4); it paralyses us so that we cannot return. It perverts us so that it captures our hearts (v. 4), and it puffs us up too (v. 5) so that we think God's forgiveness is there for us whenever we want it. How arrogant!

So God would withdraw from them (v. 6).

REFLECTION

Is that your experience? Does God seem to be distant? If he is, might it be that he's waiting for you to say 'sorry', from the heart?

DAY 10

READ Hosea 5:8–14

God is patiently waiting for his people to return to him. He's told us he's going to withdraw his affection (5:1–7). Now he shows us the second step in his strategy to cause them to come to him: he will apply discipline.

Verses 8–9 describe a military crisis. At this time Assyria, under General Tiglath-Pileser III, is on the march. When Jeroboam II, king of Israel, is succeeded by Menahem, he decides to enter into a pact with Assyria and pays them a large amount of money. This is probably what verse 13 means: 'When Ephraim [the most dominant tribe in the northern kingdom, which comes to represent the whole of the nation of Israel] saw his sickness, and Judah his sores, then Ephraim turned to Assyria, and sent to the great king for help.'

But Menahem is assassinated by Pekah, who succeeds him as king of Israel and ends the treaty with Assyria. Instead, Pekah persuades the king of Damascus to act together with him and tries to get King Ahaz of Judah to join them. But when Ahaz refuses, Pekah then invades Judah and puts Jerusalem under siege. And that simply drives Judah into the arms of Assyria, and Tiglath-Pileser III! So in a few years Assyria invades Israel and it is no more!

What does God say about all this? Read verses 12–13. God is effectively saying, 'When Assyria pounces on Israel like a lion and when disease comes to Judah, know that this is *me* coming against you!' This is startling! Sometimes God will allow us to reap the consequences of what we have sown. At other times God will actively intervene and come against us! Why? Remember his goal in verse 15.

But look at what happens in verse 13: 'When Ephraim saw his sickness and Judah his sores' ... what did he do? Astonishingly, 'then Ephraim turned to Assyria, and sent to the great king for help.' How hard it is for us to say to sorry to God! It's much easier to devise some man-made answer to our problems, in Israel's case to turn to Assyria, than to have to face up to God and seek his forgiveness.

A PRAYER

Heavenly Father, please help me not to become proud and to keep coming to you for forgiveness. Through Christ, my Lord. Amen.

DAY 11

READ Hosea 5:15 – 6:3

God is longing for his people to return to him with penitent hearts. 5:15 tells us why he will withdraw his affection (5:1–7) and send Assyria to wound them (5:8–14): 'I will go back to my place until they admit their guilt. And they will seek my face; in their misery they will earnestly seek me.' Sometimes, it is only when we've been brought really low that we will truly seek God, and it is that for which God waits.

Yet it's possible to say 'sorry' and not really mean it. In 6:1–3 scholars debate whether Israel is really serious in their confession and repentance. Are they thinking that if they are sorry for just 'two days' or a 'third' that this will win God over? Or is their contrition and repentant lifestyle one that they intend to 'press on' with? Whichever is true, God now makes clear the sort of confession for which he is looking.

He wants a frank confession of failure – they must 'admit their guilt' (5:15); there must be no more passing the buck. He wants a sincere turning of the heart towards God – 'they will earnestly seek me' (5:15); there must be no more half-hearted prayers. And he wants a humble confidence in his mercy – 'He has torn us to pieces but he will heal us; he has injured us but he will bind up our wounds' (6:1); they must look to him alone to revive and restore them.

This is the sort of apology God waits to hear. When did he last it hear it from you?

And when we do offer such a confession, we need not doubt God's forgiveness. Notice in 6:1–3 how often Hosea says, 'he will'! To people who are genuinely sorry, God will grant to them a spiritual resurrection to lift them out of the grip of sin: 'After two days he will revive us; on the third day he will restore us, that we may live in his presence' (6:2).

REFLECTION

Every one of us, even the most devoted, flirts with sin. Every one of us needs to say sorry, and to know God's reviving, life-giving Spirit within us. So in the quiet, turn to the Lord now, and sincerely confess your sin to him.

DAY 12

READ Hosea 6:4–6

Disappointment is something we all experience. There's the student who's studied hard, sat an exam and then discovers they've failed. Or there's the family who've worked hard, dreaming of their forthcoming holiday, and yet when it comes it never stops raining.

God knows disappointment too. After Israel's apology in verses 1–3, God now speaks of the frustration he feels towards them in verse 4: 'What can I do with you, Ephraim? What can I do with you, Judah?' Any parent will get to the point where they say of their child, 'I don't know what to do with him!'

This section of Hosea (from 6:4 – 7:16) describes God's disappointment with his children. Today, we focus on 6:4–6, which show us the emptiness of Israel's worship. There are three elements to it.

First, Israel blows hot and cold: 'Your love is like the morning mist, like the early dew that disappears' (v. 4). They go through their phase of loving God, but it never lasts. They can say the words of verse 3 one minute and mean them at the time, but they quickly forget them.

Second, they won't be taught: 'Therefore I cut you in pieces with my prophets, I killed you with the words of my mouth; my judgments flashed like lightning upon you' (v. 5). God repeatedly rebukes the Israelites through his prophets' words and judgments (cf. 1 Kgs. 18:21, 38–40). As a result Israel engages in a flurry of religion for a while, but then returns to idolatry again.

Third, they simply go through the motions: 'I desire mercy, not sacrifice, and acknowledgment of God rather than burnt offerings' (v. 6). Israel performs sacrifices (as the law demanded) and thinks that means God will be on their side, but God is looking for something more. Hosea keeps using the words 'mercy' and 'acknowledge' (also translated as 'knowledge'), which speak of love and commitment. God is looking for a personal relationship which lasts twenty-four hours a day, seven days a week. Years later, Jesus quoted this same verse to the Pharisees and said, 'go and learn what this means' (Mt. 9:13).

No wonder God was disappointed. Where might you be in danger of following Israel and causing God similar disappointment?

A PRAYER

Heavenly Father, I confess that so often my worship of you is superficial. I need your Spirit to change my heart. Have mercy on me, for Christ's sake. Amen.

DAY 13

READ Hosea 6:7 – 7:7

Once again you can't help feeling God's frustration with his people in the middle of our passage: 'Whenever I would restore the fortunes of my people, whenever I would heal Israel, the sins of Ephraim are exposed and the crimes of Samaria revealed' (6:11 – 7:1). It's as though God is saying, 'Whenever I try to show love to you, you go and sin again!'

If the problem in 6:4–6 was Israel's empty worship, here in 6:7 – 7:7 it's their morality. It stems from the fact that: 'Like Adam, they have broken the covenant' (6:7). God had entered into a covenant with them at Mount Sinai. He had said,

If you follow my decrees and are careful to obey my commands ... I will put my dwelling-place among you, and I will not abhor you. I will walk among you and be your God, and you will be my people (Lev. 26:3, 11–12).

Yet the people aren't living in relationship with God, so they don't care about his commands. They just do what is right in their own eyes.

So disregard for God and his authority has led to mob violence (6:8), which even the clergy get caught up in (6:9). It has led to an obsession with sex (6:10) and to dishonesty (7:1). Having forgotten God, they have no sense of any personal obligation to him or his laws. But God says, 'they do not realise that I remember all their evil deeds' (7:2). Even if they are never brought to justice on earth, God sees it all.

The kings are no better (7:3)! Verses 5–6 explain how, after the reign of Jeroboam II, king after king built his throne by killing off his rivals. With six kings dying in the space of fourteen years, it's little wonder Hosea says, 'they devour their rulers. All their kings fall' (7:7). And why? 'All their kings fall, and none of them calls on me', God, their true King, explains. The kings don't think to pray or ask God what he thinks. So, from top to bottom, the nation has lost its way morally, because it has forgotten God.

REFLECTION

Can you sense God's frustration in 6:11 – 7:1? How might you, in the way you do not obey God, be preventing yourself from knowing his restoration and healing?

A PRAYER

Heavenly Father, forgive me when I disobey you and disappoint you. Help me to follow your laws with delight, and so love to please you. For Jesus' sake. Amen.

DAY 14

READ Hosea 7:8–16

Perhaps the most hurtful thing of all about Israel's behaviour is their ingratitude towards God. So, even when they are faced with Assyria mobilising its forces and absorbing all the little nations as they march ever nearer, still Israel will not turn to God (v. 10). Instead, in their arrogance, they act as though they are some hotshot nation themselves, trying to broker a deal with the big powers of the Middle East.

Hosea now ridicules Israel. He likens them, first of all, to a pancake cooked on one side and burnt on the other (v. 8); in other words, their foreign policy is 'half-baked'. Then, because Israel thinks they are still the great Davidic empire and can cut it on the international stage, he likens Israel to an old man who refuses to accept his age (v. 9). They should have returned to God, but their arrogance blinds them (v. 10).

Israel is like a frantic dove, flying to Egypt one minute and to Assyria the next – depending on who looks strongest (v. 11). Therefore God will catch them in his net and bring them down (v. 12). God takes their dalliances with other countries personally: 'Woe to them, because they have strayed from me!' (v. 13). So he promises, 'For this they will be ridiculed in the land of Egypt' (v. 16). The very nation to whom they look for help will scorn them. That's how grieved God is. He would rather his people were laughed at than bless them in their rebellion.

Yet, notice for what God longs: 'I long to redeem them but they speak lies against me' (v. 13). He aches to hear Israel cry to him in repentance but they continue to pray to their pagan idols and 'turn away from me' (v. 14). He had 'trained them and strengthened them' but all they do is 'plot evil against me' (v. 15).

That is Israel's response to all the goodness God had shown them. How could he remain indifferent to that?

REFLECTION

Where might you be in danger of becoming arrogant? How might you be guilty of no longer crying out to God from your heart? What is your response to God's goodness to you?

A PRAYER

Heavenly Father, thank you from the bottom of my heart for redeeming me, strengthening me and training me. Help me not to arrogantly think I can do without you today. For your name's sake. Amen.

DAY 15

READ Hosea 8:1–10

Chapter 8 begins with a warning: 'Put the trumpet to your lips!' (v. 1). An eagle (or it could be 'a vulture', as the same Hebrew word is used for either bird) is about to swoop down and destroy Israel and God explains why: 'because the people have broken my covenant and rebelled against my law'. The covenant that had bound God to his people, Israel is throwing away.

Hosea knows from his own broken marriage how God feels about that kind of abandonment, and in the previous chapters he's described the pain, the disappointment and even the frustration God has borne. Now, in chapter 8, we begin to feel God's anger: 'My anger burns against them. How long will they be incapable of purity? They are from Israel!' (vv. 5–6). It beggars belief that God's people, so loved, so blessed, could have treated their relationship with him with such contempt!

Their disdain for God shows itself in Israel's self-reliance (vv. 4–10). So they appoint kings without asking God what he thinks (v. 4). People are happy to let might be right; they never consider that God's support is necessary for any government if it is to prosper.

They create their own state religion too (vv. 5–6). Hosea has spoken a lot about their worship of Baal, but here he highlights how they are worshipping two golden calves – first set up by King Jeroboam I (1 Kgs. 12:26–30) – instead of God!

Israel even sells itself, like a prostitute, to the nation that can offer them the best pact (vv. 8–9). So God will give them over to the 'mighty king' of Assyria (v. 10) – and their fortified cities will be ruined (v. 14). They will reap what they have sown (v. 7).

REFLECTION

- *Have you reached a stage in life where you believe in Christ but feel you just don't need him or rely on him, so you rely on yourself? Could God say of you, 'You've forgotten your Maker' (cf. v. 14)?*
- *What of your church? Has your church come to rely more on gifted members or money or nice buildings or good preaching, and not on God?*

Self-reliance makes God angry. If you see any trace of this in you, it would be good to turn from it now and to trust him.

A PRAYER

Heavenly Father, help me to so love you that I refuse to rely on myself. May I actively trust you in all things. In Jesus' name. Amen.

DAY 16

READ Hosea 8:11–14

The eagle (or remember it could equally be translated 'vulture') circles above the corpse of Israel (8:1). But why?

It isn't that God's temple is empty. No, as verse 2 explains, 'Israel cries out to me, "O our God, we acknowledge you."'. Was that a line from one of the temple liturgies, or perhaps an impromptu outburst from an enthusiast in the congregation? Either way it sounds spiritual enough.

It isn't that the sacrifices aren't being offered at the altar either: 'Ephraim built many altars for sin offerings' (v. 11). Moreover, 'They offer sacrifices given to me and they eat the meat' (v. 13). So they are obeying God's laws in Leviticus.

Why then is the eagle eyeing up its prey? Surely these are signs of life not decay. Well, look at the end of verse 2: 'Israel cries out to me, "O our God, we acknowledge you!" But Israel has rejected what is good.' Or read how verse 11 continues: 'Though Ephraim built many altars for sin offerings, these have become altars for sinning.' Or let the words of the rest of verse 13 sink in: 'They offer sacrifices to me, and they eat the meat, but the LORD is not pleased with them. Now he will remember their wickedness and punish their sins.'

The people say the words 'O our God, we acknowledge you', but there is no goodness in them! They bring their offerings but there is no real moral change – they had given up on the Ten Commandments long ago (v. 12). It is all religious window dressing and God will judge it. He will send them back to the place from where he rescued them: Egypt (v. 13).

God hates religious hypocrisy. So does Jesus. To the Pharisees of his day, he said: 'Woe to you ... you hypocrites! You clean the outside of the cup and dish, but inside they are full of greed and self-indulgence' (Mt. 23:25). John the Baptist put his finger on the same issue: 'And do not begin to say to yourselves, "We have Abraham as our father"', he said; rather, 'Produce fruit in keeping with repentance' (Lk. 3:8). That's what God looks for: not your words, but your life; not your singing on a Sunday, but your obedience on Monday morning. So pray for his grace that you might be real on the outside and the inside.

A PRAYER

Heavenly Father, help me to be genuine. May I not simply praise you with my lips, but would my life be obedient too. In Jesus' name. Amen.

DAY 17

READ Hosea 9:1–6

Christians have got the greatest news in the world! Out of sheer love and mercy God has forgiven us and drawn us to himself in his Son. No wonder Paul can say, 'Rejoice in the Lord always' (Phil. 4:4).

But there are times when that's the last thing God wants us to do. Hosea begins chapter 9 with just such a message: 'Do not rejoice, O Israel; do not be jubilant like the other nations' (v. 1). Perhaps the Israelites are beginning to celebrate the Feast of Tabernacles (their Harvest Festival) when, just as they're about to tuck into their food, Hosea shouts out, 'All the other nations can celebrate, but not you, Israel!'

Why would God say that? Verse 1 tells us: 'Do not rejoice, O Israel ... For you have been unfaithful to your God; you love the wages of a prostitute at every threshing-floor.' The people have compromised with false religion. They have been worshipping the pagan god Baal, which involves ritualised sex on the threshing floors during harvest. They pay money to the Baal prostitute, they perform the ritual and then they expect to get a bumper crop. The people still go to the temple and perform the sacrifices to the Lord, as we've seen in previous chapters, but they are trying to hedge their bets and think they can worship both God and Baal.

No wonder God tells the people not to come near him with their joyful songs in worship! It means nothing! Furthermore, he will make all their produce rot (v. 2), and he will evict them from the land and they will go back to being slaves, as they were in Egypt, but this time in Assyria where it will be hard to celebrate (vv. 3–4)! In fact, when the feast days come round, they will still gather together, but not for celebrations any more – just for mass burials (vv. 5–6). So God promises the land that was once fertile will soon become a wilderness (v. 6).

God is rightly jealous. As the Creator of the universe, he alone is worthy of praise. To agree with the popular view that all religions are the same might make for an easier life, but it would be a compromise. What's more, it would grieve God, who would then say to us, 'Do not rejoice!'

A PRAYER

Heavenly Father, you are the one true God, so help me to worship you alone. In Jesus' name. Amen.

DAY 18

READ Hosea 9:7–9

We saw at the beginning of chapter 9 that there are times when the very last thing God wants is for his people to rejoice. Israel's worship of Baal means that they are 'two-timing' him; their songs of praise to him are empty. But it isn't just their compromised worship that sickens God for, in verses 7–9, we discover another reason why God insists they should not rejoice.

The way the people treat his prophet and his word appals God. Hosea's marriage to Gomer the prostitute is supposed to be a sermon to the nation. Just as Hosea keeps loving his unfaithful wife, so God continues to love his unfaithful people. But the nation doesn't like it! They consider Hosea a fool, they seek to trip him up, and it is the religious leaders who give him the hardest time of all (vv. 7–8)!

It shouldn't surprise us, of course. We far prefer to hear a word that pats us on the back than one that stings, and the trouble with Hosea is that he keeps reminding Israel of their 'many' sins (v. 7). He even goes as far as to bluntly compare their present corruption with one of their most shameful past episodes: 'They have sunk deep into corruption, as in the days of Gibeah' (v. 9; you can read the sorry tale in Judg. 19:16–30). As if that isn't enough, the prophet speaks of their ultimate doom: 'the days of reckoning are at hand' (v. 7), he warns.

The point is God had sent Hosea to be a watchman (v. 8). And the watchman's job is to stand on the walls and to sound the alarm, to trumpet a warning to the nation, when he sees disaster approaching. That's what Hosea is doing, but the people would prefer someone to sing them a soothing lullaby! Tragically, they don't want to hear the word that could save them. So God insists that while they refuse to listen to his words of warning, they should not rejoice.

A PRAYER

Lord God, thank you that you love me enough to warn me. Help me to humble myself and to take to heart your Word, even when it stings, because you mean not to harm me but to make me more like Jesus. In his name. Amen.

DAY 19

READ Hosea 9:10–17

God is looking back, remembering the days when he first found Israel. You can almost hear his delight and tenderness: 'it was like finding grapes in the desert' (v. 10). Then comes the grim reality: 'But when they came to Baal Peor, they consecrated themselves to that shameful idol and became as vile as the thing they loved.' Numbers 25 relates the story of how the Israelite soldiers were enticed by the Moabite women into having sex at the local Baal shrine. The Israelites' first love for God quickly evaporated, like grapes turning sour. And now, in Hosea's day, it is happening all over again!

No wonder God's patience has run out. Time and again he has forgiven Israel and warned them, but still they persist in their unfaithfulness. So terrible punishment will ensue for Israel: their glory (God himself) 'will fly away' (v. 11) and God will 'turn away from them' (v. 12); they will become infertile (vv. 11–12), which will be ironic because Baal was supposed to be a fertility god; and war will come on them (v. 13), which will again lead to the death of their children.

As Hosea realises the horror of what God has in store, he tries to pray (v. 14). He knows things have gone too far and sin must be punished, but he longs for Israel's punishment to be softened. So, in the end, he prays for their children to never come into existence; at least then they wouldn't have to suffer such a future.

Verses 15–17 reveal God's passions. Gilgal, at the centre of Baal worship, represents the two-timing of the nation, and God hates it. Of Israel he now says, 'I will no longer love them' (v. 15) and they'll become 'wanderers among the nations' (v. 17). They will still be his people but, for a while, God is going to have to use shock treatment and withdraw his affection.

Let these red-hot words sink deep into your heart. When God loves, he loves with intensity and for keeps. Like Israel, we may offend, grieve and disappoint him. If we abandon him as our first love and continue to cheat on him, God will say to us: 'Do not rejoice' (v. 1)!

A PRAYER

Heavenly Father, thank you for your passionate love towards me. Help me never to take that love for granted and please may you always be my first love. In Jesus' name. Amen.

DAY 20

READ Hosea 10:1–8

Some people think of God as a kind old grandfather-like figure who would never do anyone any harm. He's there to smile on us and pat us on the back, they believe. The Bible's picture, however, is very different. There we discover a God who is utterly good, who burns with love, but who is passionately committed to eradicating evil and who cares enough to act. So frequently we are told to fear him.

In these verses the holy God shows up, and it's terrifying! People cry out 'to the mountains, "Cover us!" and to the hills, "Fall on us!"' (v. 8) rather than face him! I wonder if we need to learn from this? Have we so domesticated God that we can't imagine ever needing to 'fear him' in this way? If so, Hosea is showing us a side to God that we must never forget.

Three things led to God's judgment on his people. The first is their wealth. Like a flourishing vine, the nation has prospered and become fruitful (v. 1), but with money comes idolatry and a 'deceitful' or literally 'divided' heart (v. 2). Money can do that. You think you can buy anything, even God. You can't.

The second is Israel's leadership. The people swing between two extremes. In their arrogance they think they can get rid of their rulers and it doesn't matter what God thinks (v. 3). In their apathy they began to think none of their kings can be trusted (v. 4). Either way, the people have no respect for their God-appointed leaders.

Third is their place of worship. Bethel or 'Beth Aven', meaning 'house of wickedness' (v. 5) is where Jeroboam I set up the calf-idol as the centre of Israel's national religion. It has institutionalised idolatry and beguiled the people. So Hosea calls the religious leaders what they are: 'idolatrous priests'. Far from helping the nation to turn back to God, Bethel adds to the people's guilt and plunges them more rapidly into judgment.

So Israel will lose everything: their calf-idol (v. 5), their affluence (vv. 6, 8) and their leaders (v. 7). They will learn what a terrifying thing it is to fall into the hands of the living God (v. 8).

A PRAYER

Almighty and most merciful Father, teach me to fear you above anything and everything else, that I might I gain a heart of wisdom. For Jesus' sake. Amen.

DAY 21

READ Hosea 10:9–15

It could all have been so different. You hear the sad story of someone who took a wrong turning in life, or of someone who made bad choices, and you can't help wondering how things could have turned out if that step hadn't been taken or that door had remained closed.

It could all have been so different for Israel too. Terrible judgment is on its way because they refused to learn from their past. Once more Hosea refers to the terrible incident at Gibeah (v. 9; cf. 9:9), recorded in Judges 19, which had involved homosexual lust, gang rape and murder, and Israel had had to send an army to sort it out. Thousands had died. But the same things are now happening again, so God will have to send the army in once more, yet this time it will come from the 'nations' (v. 10), who will put them in chains. The trouble is Israel had simply 'remained' in their sins (v. 9) and not turned from them.

What's more, Israel has wasted so many opportunities. God had spotted Ephraim, like a farmer spots a young cow, and he had decided to harness and train it (vv. 11–12). He'd given his people chance after chance to sow seeds of righteousness, and reap the harvest of his covenant love, but they had thrown it all away: 'But you have planted wickedness,' (v. 13) says God. Instead of seeking the Lord, who stood ready to bless them, they had depended on their 'own strength' and on their 'many warriors'. So God will show them just how foolish they were to trust in military might and not in him. He will devastate all their fortresses (v. 14) and it will all be 'because your wickedness is great' (v. 15). In God's eyes it is always better to be right than to be strong.

It could all have been so different. Don't make the same mistakes that Israel made. Hosea cries out, 'it is time to seek the LORD' (v. 12). Listen to that heartfelt cry and learn.

A PRAYER

Heavenly Father, thank you that you invite me to seek you. Thank you that, in Jesus, I may truly know you and be blessed. Help me not to be like Israel, but to depend on you today. For your name's sake. Amen.

DAY 22

READ Hosea 11:1–4

We've reached one of the most poignant scenes in the whole of the Bible. Hosea shows us God alone, talking to himself. And as we hear the agonising thoughts and feelings of God, we begin to see God as a broken-hearted Father, grieving over his wayward 'son', Israel. It is a vivid picture and tenderly drawn.

Look at verse 1: 'When Israel was a child, I loved him, and out of Egypt I called my son.' Not for the first time, God is reminiscing (see 9:10, 10:1). Like a man who finds an orphaned baby boy, buys him out of slavery, adopts him and calls him 'my son', that is how God has been with Israel.

In verse 3 he remembers how he lovingly nursed his infant son, helping him to take his first faltering steps, and applying the cream to his bumps and bruises. The New English Bible puts verse 4 in this way: 'But they did not know that I harnessed them in leading-strings and led them with bonds of love – that I had lifted them like a little child to my cheek, that I had bent down to feed them.' It's a beautiful picture. Here is the Almighty God of the universe bending down to choose a people, love them, train them, care for them. Here is a generous, gentle, devoted father.

With such parenting you would have thought this child would have turned out brilliantly, wouldn't you? But listen in and discover the sad truth: 'they did not realise it was I who healed them' (v. 3). 'They don't appreciate it,' says God in effect, and 'the more I call their name, the further they go away from me and settle in the arms of other gods' (v. 2).

Perhaps you know the pain of love rejected. You can be the most considerate, loving parent, spouse or child and still your loved one turns against you. Hosea knew that. Can you believe that God knows how that feels too?

But we also learn here just how awful sin is. We tend to think of it as an impersonal breach of the rules, but that's wrong. To sin is to turn your back on the God who loves you. It is to hurt and grieve him.

A PRAYER

Almighty God, thank you that you are also my heavenly Father. Thank you for your great love to me. Help me to love you. In the name of Christ. Amen.

DAY 23

READ Hosea 11:5–7

The mood quickly changes. This gentle, tender Father now becomes furious at his son's repeated rejection:

Will they not return to Egypt and will not Assyria rule over them because they refuse to repent? Swords will flash in their cities, will destroy the bars of their gates and put an end to their plans (vv. 5–6).

God has lavished his love on Israel and all he has got in return is the cold-shoulder treatment. It is time Israel knows how that feels. He had found them in Egypt, and if they don't want him, he will send them back there. They don't want his love, so he will let them feel the sword instead.

The problem is deep-set: 'My people are determined to turn from me' (v. 7). So now if they call to God in their trouble, he will not come running. It is time for him to withdraw and to let them realise just where their choices have led them: 'Even if they call to the Most High, he will by no means exalt them.'

These are no empty words. God's anger is real, and in just a few years from when this passage was written (in 722 BC) Israel was invaded by Assyria and the people were carted off into slavery. Yes, God is a devoted Father, but that does not mean he is a pushover. In the end, he will punish all who spurn his generous love.

This means that anger in itself cannot be wrong. There are many situations where people are abused and ill-treated, and that ought to make us furious. In our anger we must not sin (Ps. 4:4), but neither must we greet injustice with disinterest.

And we must take God's anger seriously too. God loved Israel, but that didn't stop him from sending Assyria. God loves the whole world, but he still warns us of hell. Anger isn't the opposite of love; it actually arises from it. God generously offers to make us his child, just as he did Israel, but if we continually rebuff him and scorn his love, he will not simply shrug his shoulders and move on. He will be angry.

A PRAYER

Heavenly Father, I thank you that you care enough about me and your world to get angry when we reject you. Help me never to spurn your love. In Jesus' name. Amen.

DAY 24

READ Hosea 11:8–11

Deeply hurt by their spiritual adultery, God has decreed that his people will go into exile (v. 6). Yet, in his very next breath, he says,

How can I give you up, Ephraim? How can I hand you over, Israel? How can I treat you like Admah? How can I make you like Zeboiim? My heart is changed within me; all my compassion is aroused (v. 8).

Like a father wrestling over the wayward child whom he loves, God agonises over Israel.

Admah and Zeboiim were two of the cities God completely destroyed when he judged Sodom and Gomorrah. That's how strongly God feels about his people playing fast and loose with him, but he insists: 'I will not carry out my fierce anger' (v. 9). And as we listen in on God, we see the conundrum at the very heart of his character. On the one hand God cannot deny his justice, for he is just. On the other he cannot deny his mercy, for God is love. And if he were to do either of these and not the other, he would be less than God.

Humanly speaking there is no way out of this. That's why God says, 'For I am God, and not man – the Holy One among you. I will not come in wrath' (v. 9). The Roman poet Horace famously told his academy of poets: 'Never bring a god upon the stage unless your problem is such it demands a god to resolve it.' If God is to be just and loving towards his people, it will demand God himself to resolve it.

So God will send Assyria to invade Israel (v. 10), and God will be just. But unlike Admah and Zeboiim, Israel will survive and one day God will summon those he has scattered and bring them home. How could God do that? Only by coming upon the human stage himself, and out of love taking the full blow of his own justice instead of us. Hosea anticipates Jesus' sacrifice. It is only at his cross that we find that God can be love and utterly just, and neither is compromised. The anger that we deserve for betraying him, he took in Christ for us, and all that remains is his love towards us.

A PRAYER

Heavenly Father, thank you so much for sending Jesus and for the cross, where wrath and mercy meet. Amen.

DAY 25

READ Hosea 11:12 – 12:6

We've reached the final four chapters of Hosea's prophecy which rehearse the themes of the book: Israel's spiritual adultery (11:12 – 12:14) and the divine anger they've aroused (13:1–16), yet God's longing for a renewed relationship (14:1–9).

Chapter 12 begins with Israel's unfaithfulness. How have they offended God? By living deceitfully: 'Ephraim has surrounded me with lies, the house of Israel with deceit' (11:12). Judah (in the south) is little better, but Israel has tried to live a double life.

This has shown itself in their relationship with God. They've sought to follow the Lord, but they've continued to worship the pagan deities too. Notice how, by contrast, Hosea refers to the One that Israel has sought to deceive! He is 'the faithful Holy One' (11:12). What he says, he does. When he makes a promise, he keeps it.

It's also shown itself in Israel's foreign policy. On the one hand they've tried to keep Assyria happy and made a 'treaty' with them, and on the other they've sent 'olive oil to Egypt' (12:1). They should have fed on God's Word (Deut. 8:3), but instead they've fed on the wind, whichever way they thought it was blowing. At every level they've been deceitful. Ultimately it will be futile too (like eating the wind!).

Hosea turns to Judah (though Israel remains in his sights). In many ways they are like their forefather, Jacob (12:2–6). He had been the past master of deceit, grasping his older brother's heel (12:3; cf. Gen. 25:26) and snatching his inheritance, all the while pretending to be Esau (cf. Gen. 27). And yet God had managed to turn that 'grasping' around and make it a blessing. It had been at Bethel (12:4; notice Hosea uses its real name, not the nickname 'Beth Aven' this time) that Jacob had been humbled and changed (cf. Gen. 28:10–22).

God holds out the possibility of doing the same again all these years later with Jacob's descendants (12:6). If only they would learn from their forefather and return to God and not to a golden calf, they too would have a future. It was, after all, the Lord who had brought about the reversal in Jacob's fortunes and no-one else (12:5).

A PRAYER

Heavenly Father, thank you that you can turn a Jacob into an Israel. Please do that change in me. For Jesus' sake. Amen.

READ Hosea 12:7–14

Hosea is shining the spotlight on Israel's double life, their infidelity, which has so grieved God. Yet their pretence at devotion to Yahweh (while worshipping other gods) and their duplicity in foreign affairs (courting Egypt while flirting with Assyria) are not their only crimes, as verses 7–9 show.

The sad truth is that Israel, God's 'son' (11:1), has turned out just like all the other kids. Israel has become like the 'merchant' (literally 'Canaanite') who 'uses dishonest scales' and 'loves to defraud' (v. 7). When God had brought Israel up out of Egypt (v. 9) and had given them the land that was occupied by the wicked Canaanites, he had said to them,

Do not defile yourselves in any of these ways, because this is how the nations that I am going to drive out before you became defiled. Even the land was defiled; so I punished it for its sin, and the land vomited out its inhabitants (Lev. 18:24-25).

Israel was supposed to have been a distinct, different and holy nation (cf. Ex. 19:5–6). Instead, they have simply copied all the dishonest practices of the peoples around them. They have become like the world.

Their dishonesty has made them wealthy, and their riches have made them arrogant and blind (v. 8). It's a well-worn path. Years later the Laodiceans went the same way (cf. Rev. 3:17–19), and the result was a church which make the Lord Jesus sick.

Israel's sins have made God feel the same way. They have provoked his anger (v. 14). If the only way he can shock them into repentance is to evict them from the land and make them into a nomadic people once again, he will do it (v. 9). Their religiosity will not save them (v. 11). If they think, like their father Jacob, they can devise their own clever schemes and that they no longer need God to secure their promised blessing (v.12, cf. Gen. 27) they will have another thing coming. It could all have been so different if they had only listened to the prophets God had sent them all down the years to warn them, to rescue them and to care for them (vv. 10, 13). But God's people had ignored God's Word and gone their own merry way. They would now pay for their sins (v. 14).

A PRAYER

Heavenly Father, help me to be yours, holy and distinct. For Jesus' sake. Amen.

DAY 27

READ Hosea 13:1–3

With this penultimate chapter comes the darkest part of Hosea's prophecy. God's fierce anger towards his unchaste bride is given full vent. But it comes, once more, as God looks back on Israel's past.

In just a few words (in vv. 1–3) Hosea manages to sketch Israel's demise. He moves swiftly from the past (v. 1), to the present (v. 2) to the future (v. 3). There was a time when Ephraim (the dominant tribe in the north) spoke and all the other tribes and surrounding nations sat up and listened, but Hosea traces the moment when Israel sowed the seeds of their own downfall back to when they turned from Yahweh (the source of their life and strength) to worshipping Baal instead (v. 1). At that point, even though they continued to exist, it was as if the relationship with God had 'died' (and the people with it).

Stepping away from the living God and towards idolatry, they had started something which they couldn't control. Their flirtations became addictive and gave birth to more and more sin (v. 2). They now find themselves in the ridiculous situation of their highly skilled craftsman making cows for people to kiss! It would be laughable if it wasn't so tragic.

So God promises that in the future this once great kingdom will go up in smoke (v. 3). It will be like the morning mist or the dew, which quickly evaporates; like the husk around the wheat that is blown away by the wind, Israel will disappear.

And they did. In just a few years (722 BC) the 'east wind' (13:15) of the Assyrian military machine would blow in and take everything – both goods from their 'storehouse' and their 'treasures' (the capital city of Samaria was known for its affluence) as well as people. Even the possibility of future generations would be removed as the soldiers slaughtered pregnant women (13:16).

All this would happen because the people had 'rebelled against their God' and 'must bear their guilt' (13:16) Israel fell not because they were poor, nor because Assyria was stronger, but because they abandoned the Lord and chased after Baal. Walking away from God only brings death and our own demise.

A PRAYER

Heavenly Father, thank you that you are the source of life and love, of strength and goodness. Help me to love you and not flirt with anyone or anything else which might threaten my devotion to you. In Jesus' name. Amen.

READ Hosea 13:4–12

What arouses God's anger? We've seen Israel's unfaithfulness – how they went after Baal or the calf-idols (vv. 1–3); that certainly did it.

But it isn't just idolatry. Pride provokes God's anger too. He had heard Israel's cries in Egypt and had saved them (v. 4). The people had stood at Mount Sinai and heard God say, 'You shall have no other gods before me' (Ex. 20:3), and they'd been showered with gifts as he had provided for them and met their every need (v. 5). No other nation had known the privileges that Israel had. But the more God gave them, the more highly they thought of themselves and their own abilities (v. 6). They quickly forgot God, thinking they didn't need him, and that pride and ingratitude made him furious! He may have been like a father or a husband in the past, but Israel will soon see him in a very different guise. He will turn on them like some ferocious predator – as a lion, a leopard or a bear (vv. 7–8).

Idolatry and pride kindle God's wrath, as does one more thing: unbelief. Israel will be destroyed because instead of trusting God (their 'helper', v. 9), they had wanted a king to believe in. God had allowed, in his law, for the nation to have a king (cf. Deut. 17:14–20), but they'd wanted one for all the wrong reasons. You can read the sorry tale in 1 Samuel 8. They wanted a military leader who could secure their future: 'a king to lead us, such as all the other nations have' (1 Sam. 8:5). God saw it for what it was: 'they have rejected me as their king' (1 Sam. 8:7). He had nevertheless given them what they'd asked for, but where has it got them? Their monarch has become little more than a puppet of the Assyrian empire! If only they'd looked not to their 'king' or 'rulers' (v. 10) but to 'the LORD your God' (v. 4).

God has been so patient, but Israel's record of continued idolatry, pride and unbelief cannot be ignored (v. 12). In the end, God's anger will burn against them and they will feel it.

A PRAYER

Heavenly Father, thank you that you are far more patient than I could ever be, but may I never take that patience for granted. Help me to run from sin. For Jesus' sake. Amen.

DAY 29

READ Hosea 13:13–16

Just as we begin to think that Israel's sin is so great and God's anger so furious that the nation's end is certain, Hosea surprises us. In the dying words of this chapter, hope begins to flicker once more.

Hosea cries, 'Pains as of a woman in childbirth come to him' (v. 13)! The sufferings that Israel is about to endure as the Assyrians invade need not be the last twinges before death; they could be the pains of childbirth! The situation before God's people doesn't have to be terminal; life could still be snatched even from the jaws of death. The only trouble is Israel's obstinacy: 'but he is a child without wisdom; when the time arrives, he does not come to the opening of the womb.'

So, because Israel will not be 'reborn', because they choose the grave, God says,

I will have no compassion ... An east wind from the LORD will come, blowing in from the desert ... They will fall by the sword; their little ones will be dashed to the ground, their pregnant women ripped open (vv. 14–16).

If only Israel would wisely choose life, but their stubborn refusal means this will be their last chance.

Yet, even though this generation chooses death, God will not give up on his people: 'I will ransom them from the power of the grave; I will redeem them from death' (v. 14). Israel might be faithless, but God had committed himself to them at Sinai (13:4), and when he makes a promise he keeps it, no matter what. The Apostle Paul knew that. As he writes about God's ultimate triumph over our greatest enemies of sin and death and hell, it's to these words that he turns:

When the perishable has been clothed with the imperishable, and the mortal with immortality, then the saying that is written will come true: 'Death has been swallowed up in victory.' 'Where, O death, is your victory? Where, O death, is your sting?' (1 Cor. 15:54–55).

Hosea knows more than anyone that God's love for his people never gives up. It was he who'd been told by God to: 'Go, show your love to your wife again, though she is loved by another and is an adulteress' (3:1). God had made it very clear – Hosea was to: 'Love her as the LORD loves the Israelites' (3:1). For the Israelites death and hell might seem to threaten God's love, but in truth it is invincible. That is the grace of God, and therein lies our hope.

A PRAYER

Heavenly Father, thank you that your love never gives up, that it is unconquerable. In Jesus' name. Amen.

DAY 30

READ Hosea 14:1–3

Chapter 13 concluded with chilling words. God had been incredibly patient with Israel. He'd sent prophet after prophet to warn them about their persistent unfaithfulness, but time had run out, and now he had to act. And so in 722 BC the Assyrians swept in and destroyed the capital, Samaria.

The question is: Had God finished with Israel? And it's chapter 14 which provides the answer. Judgment has fallen and now, as the dust settles, God sends Hosea with a message. Look at verse 1: 'Return, O Israel, to the LORD your God. Your sins have been your downfall!' Notice how Hosea calls God 'your God'! It's an astonishing invitation! Despite everything, he will still have them back. In fact, he's waiting for them to return. Of course they will have to come not with empty sacrifices (as they had for so many years in the temple) but with serious words of apology (v. 2) and repentance (v. 3). They must approach too with a determination to walk away from their past: 'We will never again', and also from thinking they could save themselves: 'what our own hands have made'.

And what will they find when they go back to him? A Father of compassion (v. 3) who longs to take care of the needy (as v. 4 in tomorrow's section will make explicit). I don't know about you, but I find that utterly astonishing. The words at the end of chapter 13 might well have sent a shiver down our spine, and they ought to have, for rebelling against God is not 'nothing'; it is utterly serious and God can't ignore it. But these words in verses 1–3 are those God far prefers to say; this is where his heart lies, that even after judgment he longs for his people to come back to him. Like the father looking, waiting, aching for his son's homecoming, so God yearns for us to return.

It says something about our pride and stubbornness that it took a national disaster to bring Israel to the point where they could pray a prayer like this and mean it, doesn't it? How much tragedy might God have to bring into your life before you're willing to approach him with similar words of humility, honesty and genuine sorrow?

A PRAYER

Gracious Father, thank you that in spite of all my sin, you long for me to be with you. Help me to remember that. For Jesus' sake. Amen.

DAY 31

READ Hosea 14:4–9

We've reached the end of our love story. Was Hosea's marriage to Gomer ever restored, properly? The prophet doesn't tell us. What we do know is that the love story that Hosea's marriage was supposed to reflect still goes on, for the God of Israel is the God and Father of the Lord Jesus and he is determined to have a people for himself, whatever they've done.

Listen again to his appeal: 'Return, O Israel, to the LORD your God' (14:1). Hear now his promise to those who come: 'I will heal their waywardness and love them freely, for my anger has turned away from them' (v. 4). God is determined to love his people, and if they're incapable of remaining faithful, his strength will supply their weakness, he 'will heal their waywardness'.

So God's love will be the key to Israel finding new life. Like the dew it will refresh them and enable them to blossom (v. 5). The nation, now broken, will once again stand tall (vv. 5–6) and will prosper (v. 7) under God's care (v. 8): 'your fruitfulness comes from me'.

The trouble is that after the Assyrian invasion Israel was no more. Judah survived for a bit longer, but was then conquered by the Babylonians. Eventually some of God's people came back and resettled, but the nation was only a poor reflection of what it had once been. And yet the faithful clung to verses like these, believing that one day God's promises would come true. And they did. In Jesus God himself burst onto the scene and promised life in all its fullness for Israel and Judah, for Jew and Gentile. Life would come, but only as Jesus embraced death and turned the anger of God away from us. Three days later, as Jesus rose from the dead and shattered the death barrier, he proved that there is nothing as unconquerable as God's love. When he promises, 'I will … love them freely', he means it, whatever the cost.

Hosea ends with a postscript in verse 9. He doesn't want any of his words to go to waste. So be wise before God and determine to act on what you've learned.

A PRAYER

Heavenly Father, thank you for all that Hosea has taught me about your persistent, never-giving-up, all-conquering love. I know that love was costly. Help me to love you truly. For Jesus' sake. Amen.

MORE IN THIS SERIES

ROMANS
Momentous News
By David Cook
ISBN: 978-1-906173-24-1

MARK
The Suffering Servant
By Jeremy McQuoid
ISBN: 978-1-906173-55-5

DANIEL
Far From Home
By Justin Mote
ISBN: 978-1-906173-68-5

1 THESSALONIANS
Living for Jesus
By Julia Marsden
ISBN: 978-1-906173-67-8

PHILIPPIANS
Press Towards the Goal
By Kay Mumford
ISBN: 978-1-909611-31-3

GALATIANS
The Life I Now Live
By Peter Mead
ISBN: 978-1-910587-09-6

ACTS
To the Ends of the Earth
By David Cook
ISBN: 978-1-909611-02-3

EZEKIEL
For His Glory
By Peter Lau
ISBN: 978-1-909611-83-2

JOHN
Never Thirst Again
By David Cook
ISBN: 978-1-909611-30-6

and more at... 10 Publishing
a division of 10 of those.com

To place an order call: **0844 879 3243** email: **sales@10ofthose.com**
or order online: **www.10ofthose.com**

David Gibb
HOSEA
31 UNDATED DEVOTIONS THROUGH THE BOOK OF HOSEA